Just a Moment

Stephen Mallick

Just a Moment

Acknowledgement is due to the following publications,
in which some of these poems have previously appeared:
Overland, *Quadrant*, *Redoubt*, *Westerly* and *Famous Reporter*.

For
Suzanne, Sophie, Sam and Joe

Just a Moment
ISBN 978 1 74027 532 3
Copyright © text Stephen Mallick 2008

First published 2008
Reprinted 2016

Ginninderra Press
PO Box 3461 Port Adelaide SA 5015
www.ginninderrapress.com.au

Contents

Perfume Bottle	7
Grafting	8
The Nest	9
Three Small Poems	10
Before School	11
Cannibal	12
Carcass	13
The Dam	14
Fig Tree	15
North-West Bay	16
Rabbits	17
First Kill	18
Bird Feeding	19
Rumours	20
The Devil's Books	21
Boils to Lance: A Personal Helicon	22
The Marriage Tree	23
Golf	24
Drama	25
Evening	26
Mon Frère	27
Eldest	28
Regret	29
Twin Taps	30
Service	31
A Bird Sang	32
Veranda Lace	33
Wood Chopping	34
Poet's Wife	35
Fetching Wood	36

Kiss	37
One Afternoon	38
Books	39
Pet	40
Bequest	41
Lunch	42

Perfume Bottle

One Christmas I remember, but not
For joy. My father's present
Thrilled us all. We watched, as from
Its nest of coloured crepe she drew –

A perfume bottle. The pear-shaped
Vial was amber in the light,
A glass grenade. Months later
I found it, still in its box, untouched.

Grafting

We used to own a bit of orchard.
Nothing much – a patch of turf
Where ancient fruit trees curtsied yearly,
Bowed down by crops of thick-skinned fruit.

Like Chinese lanterns the apples hung.
And if the peel was tough as rind,
With scabs, and scales, and pimply knobs
Like carbuncles, I didn't mind

When the flesh was sweet. But most had worm,
Or wrinkled early on the tree;
Still full of sap too thinly spread,
We had to call the grafter in.

I watched his work, paring limbs
With razor knives, slicing the core
To fit a bud of new wood cut
From a foreign tree, then trussing all

With tape. And watched, and feared at first
That both – the new and old – were doomed.
Then the sap fused, the fibres stuck,
And the little green nodules bloomed.

The Nest

Walking home from school through the back blocks
We found within a clump of box, a nest
That held as in a palm three tiny eggs.
Above us whirred the chatter of the hen;
Perching nearby on a twig, she hopped
And sang and bent her needle eye on us.

Disturbed, we went away. And when it chanced
We came that way again, in pairs or threes,
We gave the place a decent berth. But once
I came alone and peering in, a cry
And sudden bolt of feathers made me cringe.
I thought I was blinded, and ran away,
Slipping and falling and bruising myself but never
Stopping till I'd gained the yard, where I paused
To wipe my face and curse my fears.

Three Small Poems

I

After a week of expectation, mother
Stripped and set the cut to thaw and puddle
Weak red blood beside the sink. The oven
Streamed as blooming onions browned in fat.
Then she'd nick a slice for us to taste, mix
Milk with the sump, and bake Yorkshire pudding
For our Sunday roast.

II

Just like us, they paired for ever, never
Changed their minds. Marching about like proud
White-cassocked priests, while ducks and chickens
Scratched for feed, they'd roll their anxious eyes
And snap and strut and, arching slender necks
Into a warning, hiss, 'How dare you, sir,
Look down on a goose.'

III

It marred the whole week, threw a long shadow
From Thursday to Tuesday. Wednesdays as my friends
Took seats for home, and smiled and waved, I ached
With envy. Four o'clock was the hanging hour.
The room was always cool and dark, the white
Keys gleamed, as from the hall I heard the knell
For my piano lesson.

Before School

Big bony haunches, legs
Like skittles, her belly distended
And blotched, with soft orb eyes
Protruding and scanning your hand
For food, and rubbery lips –
She wasn't much to look at.

Then we noticed the change.
Her udder got bigger, a tight
Pink bag full of milk, teats
As long as your fingers and wrinkled.

One morning our father called us.
A solemn occasion we stood
Quietly watching her straining.
A little blood flowed, she bleated
But 'No!' he said. 'You can't help her.'

Then she dropped to her knees, her eyes
Bulging. A leg kicked out,
In a rush the rest of it came.

It shocked me that something so
Large could emerge, to flop
Sloppily onto the sand.
Then another. Sickened, I turned
Away to trail all day
A bloody white slime, no one knew.

Cannibal

So warm and cloud-soft, their pink eyes
Glazed with indifference, asleep
In straw or daintily feeding on scraps:
They were as innocent as myself.

When one grew fat. So I caged the male,
The big brute who would eat the young.
And watched him carefully, tried to
Surprise the hate he must have felt;
For in his eyes I could detect, not
Fear, just a cold desire for blood.

It was him I teased, withheld his food,
Made life a misery. Until the doe,
The loving mother ate the young
And left a spot of blood behind to show
The deed, that nothing in her eye revealed.

Carcass

In one corner of a soggy cornfield,
Under a lichen-tufted fence post,
A patch of blackened ground
Ringed with tall foxgloves:

Old bones, a tent of old skin,
The skull a few feet off in the briar.
With a long stick I poked around
In the embers of that slow fire.

The Dam

For Peter Rand

I loved the rain, for when the gutters sobbed
And spilled in runnels down the sand, its level
Would rise up like a lump in your throat. In summer
It sank, and dried and chapped, and we'd arrive
With boots and borrowed spades to sink our shafts
Downward, deeper and deeper, mining for clays.
The rust-clay for building; the green
That killed you if you touched it; and the white,
The pure vein, bone-white, more precious than gold.

Then one morning I heard the purr
Of tractors, and shouts of men. They'd come
To clear and subdivide the land.
Breakfast done, we visited
To find a muddy naked patch.
How it filled me with a sense of power
To see the earth disclosed like that.

Just then they cut the dyke in two.
Mounting to the lip we stood
And watched our dam bleed to death.
Its slimy sides all pitted and gashed
Gave up their mystery. There was nothing there,
A gaping hole, the mud
Pus-coloured, and stinking, too.

Fig Tree

Twenty-five foot it towered
Over our house, a granddaddy of a tree,
Its bulging trunk as broad as a door
Bifurcating out of the dark soil, it was
Rooted way down in the earth. I loved it.

Already the little green globes were sprouting
All over. It would be a fine crop that year.
And by March the blushing had started.
The green fruit swelled, like smooth fat cysts, turned
Purple and split. They were ready for picking.

A fig tree isn't easy to climb. Twigs
Scratch and whip, in the sap is a poison
Brings out red weals on the skin.
Yet climb and pick I did,

Filled buckets, trays, kitchen bowls and pots
Till everything hollow was bursting. And still
There were more. Of the overripe ones
I boiled up potful after potful of jam,
An army of bottles that conquered the house.
All my friends received gifts. Some I asked over
To pick a load for themselves.
They came, picked; departed. Still there were more.

Disregarded they ripened, fermenting
There on the branch, fell on cement
With a dull plop. The jam, too,
Went uneaten, acquired a fur of mould
Like a first soft beard on the top.

North-West Bay

For Cameron Williams

I have been back, and all our dreams were there.
The polished stones and weedy banks, the brown
Stream, the muddy flats and fields, the gates:
All there. Nothing changed. And in a pool
That recognised me, I recognised a face.

Spring mornings were the best of all.
Beneath the pressure of our boots the earth
Gave up in spurts of mud imaginings
That lived and breathed. We'd shun the road,
Skirt homesteads, cross a field of corn, then strike
Up-river, keeping always near the banks.
On either side bald paddocks rolled to a rim
Of bush: but where the yellow willows clung
And flotsam clung to willows, all was safe.

Up to a certain spot. A shining pool,
Soft as a cow's eye, opened there;
But by the weir the water deepened
To a pupil filled with violent space. I feared it
As I fear the dark. You feared it, too,
And together we never could pass that place.

Rabbits

We spent our lunch time reading things that grew
Into experience; of loops of thread
Too thin to see for snaring hares; of how
You clubbed escaping young ones on the head.

The shaggy bush and ragged paddocks jarred.
But then we'd dreamed so fervently, the fat
Cows, the sheep, and even distant flocks
Of starlings thrilled us. With the staves we'd cut

From gums we flushed the scrub, until the sun
Cooled our lust. Then, hopeful still, but tired
With talk of killing we shouldered our guns
And bags expertly, went home satisfied.

Till we met Scot Hanson with his brothers
Coming along by the river, a swag
Of fat rabbits strung on a wire. We grew
Up then, cursed our airguns, our empty hands.

First Kill

The warm day received us, plunged knee-deep
In heather we crested the hill, left the safe ground
Behind. Left relations, our old selves, all.
The smooth feel of the stock, the faint smell
Of oil, the ripe look of a cartridge. No –
I've never known a full manhood like that.

The heather grew scanty. Old blistered gums
Clutched at our barrels, tired to wrest them
From our hands. I didn't know that the bush
Has a voice. I heard only silence, the dry
Crunch of our boots on the stones. If the bush
Has a voice, if it cares for its children,
Then why didn't it speak? If it did
I heard nothing, I swear I heard nothing.

Their strange cries, part human part
bird reached us first then like
sparks of green fire they
darted in sight. I trained on
one, saw the surprise of its
body as I let in the light.
Then it fell like a stone.

Stone-dead? No, it throbbed on the ground, one eye
Cocked on my rifle. I loaded: it knew me.
Then I finished it off. Without life in its eye
A warm bundle of feathers that drooped in my hand.
But something had snapped, with that first kill.

Bird Feeding

A wattlebird, feeding on
Our proteas, balanced a moment, rocking
As it raped the flower. It was eager,
Very intent, and I thought, guilty
Of something obscene. There was science in the way
Its blunt nail of a beak stabbed and withdrew
And stabbed again, all in a twinkling.
Such a brutal operation, and so quick.

Then it was over, the bird flung off the flower
That was dancing wildly in recoil. It was still
When I reached it, as though nothing had happened.
I could find no sign of damage, each pistil
Intact, no tears in the soft tissue
That was pink, and immaculate. I wondered then
Was the desecration mine, having watched?

Rumours

My brother and his friends met in
His room, and remained there all day:
Doing what? We looked for signs,
Got just another 'Go away!'

So we sulked about the yard, and watched
The door, then snuck in stealthily
When they left: a stuffy smell, botched
Fags, and soccer magazines.

With once a gem hidden among
The dross, its greasy corners dark
With the prints of countless thumbs.
We fingered it, too, left our marks.

The Devil's Books

The rhythm of the middle-morning broken
By a call: 'All grades assemble, please.'
We trickled out, glad enough to take
A break, when the yard's glare struck forcefully

And we lined up in silence. The principal,
His mike in one hand, held aloft what looked
Like magazines. A menial approached
With fuel in a can, cast down the Devil's Books

And doused them. Sunlit-pale the pyre
Peeled away in ribbons, leaving ash,
Which he stamped on and scattered. No one
Smiled. But I recalled the perfect flesh.

Boils to Lance: A Personal Helicon

After Seamus Heaney

On the neck, the buttocks and over the back
They appeared, as little pimples that glazed
At the edges, then went hard as a tack:
Tender nipples that hurt when you squeezed.

We were dirtier than other families, went
With our feet bare, in odd-coloured clothes,
Soiled collars and caps: and sensed
The difference, as from this we acquired

The good habit of pride. But boils are a curse
And, each spring, we had a ritual lancing.
My mother officiated. A cold-blooded nurse,
She bathed the offending spot with a lotion

That scalded the skin, till there was a glow
Of pus, which she burst. It was murder.
I gritted my teeth, made a brave show,
But what I remember is pain, not pleasure.

The Marriage Tree

It was summer, early morning, about seven
When she told me. She took me into the garden
And under a tree, a weeping acacia, told me.

It was an ugly tree, scraggy, with dead pods
Like withered testicles, and not many leaves.
Years later I cut it back to its roots –
The wood was pasty-coloured and sour –
Chopped the trunk into lengths
To fit the hearth. And kindled the rest.

Long burnt. But the news has remained,
Like a dormant seed still sometimes flowers
Inside me. But today it bears a sweeter fruit.

Golf

He shook my proffered hand, firm,
His palm dry and papery, just
As I remembered it, and turned
To shoulder-up his bag of clubs.

In his prime he'd shot a par
Of single figures, practising
On the sandy greens of New South Wales.
Now, although he had his swing

Still, the strength was gone. I played
Easy, but beat him easily.
He was proud, and rather hurt, and went
To buy the drinks, leaving me

To check the card. I watched the trees
Sway, the coloured trousers dance
About the green, and wished
He'd triumphed, as he had done once.

Drama

See that old man, there
In the sun, closed eyes
Watching his life's reel
Unwind: only the last act
Remains, the denouement
Resolving nothing.
There was love, many
Great scenes in which he
Starred. The plot moved
Quickly, welcomes
Following hard on the heels
Of farewells, till the list
Of credits grew too long
To memorise, was at last
Discarded. Now the script's
Monologue, the voice
Growing softer and wiser
With each phrase. The end
Is uncertain, either complete
Silence, or perhaps
One final dialogue.

Evening

In the evening when I come
Unannounced, you rise from your chair
By the phone, flustered but happy.
I take my usual place, opposite,
And wait for you to speak. You don't.
Having dispensed with words you just
Light a cigarette, and sit
Observing through a screen of smoke.
You puff, and sigh, then stub the butt,
And light another to observe
Me through another screen. You think
You see deeply. Perhaps you do.
The weight of books above your head
Is impressive, but I've read them too.

Mon Frère

Cut from the same stump, you and I.
I podded in the damp soil: you
Had little time for that. I lingered:
You made plans, enacted, did the things
Young men do, in the best ways,
Without fuss. I had so many
False starts, while you just
Went on growing, back straight, eyes
Fixed on the sun. So what are you –
A man of action, in the first rank.
But epithets don't do you justice.
Another man, yes, but not you.
Weren't we cut from the same stump
By the same hands, the same axe?

Eldest

I saw your eldest, buying
Milk, and hailed him: he
Came, but slowly, I thought
For a friend's son. He's yours

By the eyes, but his mother's life
Kept swimming to the surface
Of the pupil, which
Narrowed then and judged me.

Regret

She lived down that street – so I believe.
I never saw the actual house,
Never knew which number marked the place
Where, had I been a bit more bold,
I might have loved and found relief.

I haven't forgotten, twenty years on;
A fresh crime yet, after all this time.
I did wrong, yes, but not to her –
She'd laugh if she bothered to remember
A boy whose mother was too strong.

Twin Taps

I watch two taps dripping:
One is quick and sure.
The other hesitates,
Then lets fall also.

I hear a conversation;
One voice is bold,
The other diffident
But not cold;

And imagine they're at odds –
Twin set against twin.
When two drops falling
Make one.

Service

It's easy to pray, in some
Places. The sea, for instance
Is conducive to prayer. Silence
Helps, and wide open spaces;

Sunlight on an opposite hill
When your own is in shadow.
Deserts have always been suitable
But scarce. Closer to home

There is the dawn, the stillness
Of a deserted house. Death
And birth, both old favourites.
Churches are built for prayer:

Each Sunday, sometimes
Weekdays they do service.
I, too, can pray
In churches, when they're empty.

A Bird Sang

When I stepped out, a bird sang –
I believed it was for me.
His song broke out just as I
Was passing under him.

When I returned – it wasn't long –
I paused at the door
For him to sing, to say goodnight.
He offered nothing more.

Veranda Lace

The new lace looks lovely,
Lovelier than we'd hoped.
Today as I came in
From a long day worn thin
I had to smile at how quaint it looked.

Yes, the old house had a fresh look
With just this trifling ornament.
And I was pleased,
And a little uneased
To have gained such establishment.

Wood Chopping

Of all night sounds, I love the thwack
and fall of a wood block,
and the gentler knock
as it's thrown on the stack.

And my nearest neighbour's half-muffled talk
as he pauses to breathe,
then again heaves
for another crack.

And the ripple of the echo
of his labour done.
And when this dies,
and I listen: nothing.

Poet's Wife

She was never mentioned, at least
Not directly. There was too much to say,
About the wind, how it moved the leaves
Of emotion, this way and that way;
About life's frosts; how the young shoots
Perished for want of shelter,
How the early fruit, bruised by hail
And coarse rain, fell and was wasted.
Only when all this had been said
Many times; when the new grafts
Were taking and the old wounds healing;
Only when the dormant seed
Was at last made good, only then.

Fetching Wood

It's getting on for nine o'clock.
I've eaten: the kitchen's warm and safe, and were
I outside looking in must seem
A golden cave. The fire's troubled
By the wind, but no wind troubles here.

My wife prepares for bed. I watch.
Absorbed as a nun about her prayers
She slaps by softly on the tile.
Somewhere water kicks the pipe;
A silence, followed by a sob
Of water. She'll brush a hundred times
Each side, apply her creams, and passing
Bid me stoke the fire for night.

The nightsky glistens, and the stars
Shake above me as I go
Down the yard to where the woodpile
Hunches obscure in shadow. The smell
Of grass crushed by my boots rises,
Reminding me how as a child
I would have hurried, scraping shins,
And picked up wet wood. Now, I pause
Then gather up the rough bundles
Slowly, loving their living inertness
Against the insides of my arms.

I secure the door, and kill the lights;
The darkened kitchen opens on
The fire. I open the gate to stoke it
And stand back to watch it throb
Into knew life. Then damp the flue.
Dwindled it'll last the night.

Kiss

Smell her hair! Sweet, untrammelled
As mountain water infused with light.
Stroke it. Softer than a cloud,
Finer than a puff of sunshine, pure
As quartz. Kiss it, quickly,
This head has known no dark thoughts.

One Afternoon

I went back, to a hill
Rioting with flowers, tangled
Heather, and peppermint gums;
Everything just the same.

I brought nothing, no key
With which to interpret, no wisdom
I didn't have then. Nothing
But you to sit with me.

Books

I remember the day
I dropped in for a look
At the stiff competition,
The new poetry books.

I had you with me,
And to keep you calm
I plunked you down
In the kids section.

Then wandered off
To my two shelves,
Between the biographies
And the novels.

Familiar stuff,
Old names, some new:
I looked at the publishers,
Opened a few;

Then turned away,
Sick at heart;
Dreary words,
A dead art.

And found you reading –
How can I explain?
I felt things stirring
Once again.

Pet

Your first, you hardly knew
If you loved it at all,
Only when it escaped, wouldn't
Come when you called.

Then cruelty came natural
As love flowed before;
That you felt both together
And suffered, I saw

But withheld my censure:
Let innocence partake
Of humiliation, then love
Again for pity's sake.

Bequest

From all the things
Jumbled in there,
The imitations
And old decorations,
The pearl necklaces
And signet rings,
(Though you'd never
Seen it before)
You picked it out;
The thin chain your mother,
And her mother, wore.

Lunch

For baby birds, a tiny meal of soaked bread,
An up-turned jar lid for a water trough:
They huddled in their messed shavings,
Fearful, resigned to the inevitable.

For orphaned field mice, I tried
Delicate titbits, of bacon rind
Chopped fine, and breadcrumbs:
They refused to eat, to save themselves.

And one wild gull, her diseased leg
Reduced to a knarled lump,
Hopped and croaked about the wire pen,
Would never eat what I gave her.

Waiting at the school gate, thinking
Of vulnerable, defenceless things;
Of small hopes, smaller failures;
Of my own, unopened lunch box.

www.ingramcontent.com/pod-product-compliance
Lightning Source LLC
Chambersburg PA
CBHW062206100526
44589CB00014B/1985